THE SECRETS OF INSOMNIA: SELF-TRAINING FOR HEALING,

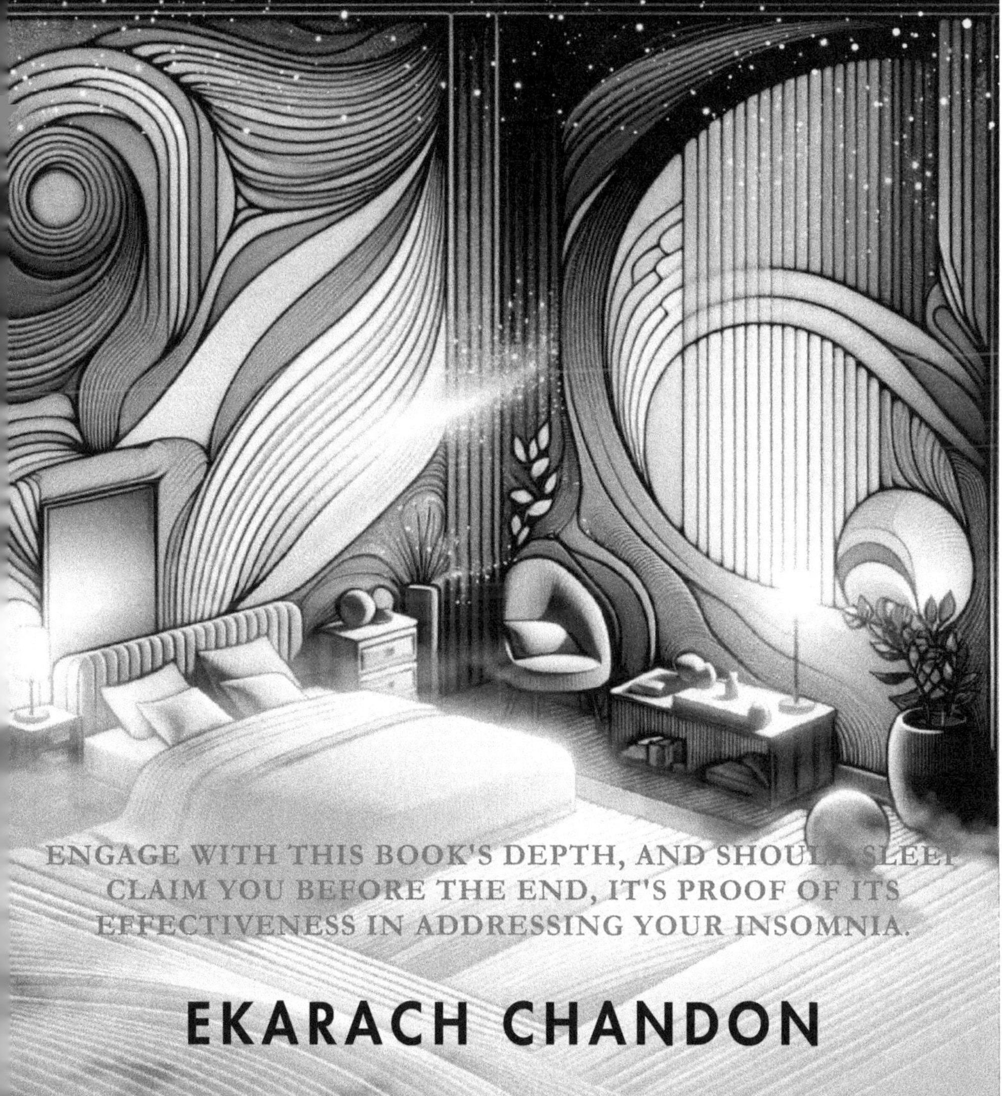

ENGAGE WITH THIS BOOK'S DEPTH, AND SHOULD SLEEP CLAIM YOU BEFORE THE END, IT'S PROOF OF ITS EFFECTIVENESS IN ADDRESSING YOUR INSOMNIA.

EKARACH CHANDON

EKARACH CHANDON

THE SECRETS OF INSOMNIA: SELF-TRAINING FOR HEALING,

GUIDED STRATEGIES FOR OVERCOMING SLEEPLESSNESS

THE SECRETS OF INSOMNIA: SELF-TRAINING FOR HEALING,

THE MAIN THEMES OF BOOK SERIES

DERIVATIVE KNOWLEDGE APPLIED TRUTH FROM NEW THOUGHT: A PRACTICAL GUIDE TO UNLOCKING TRUTH FROM NEW THOUGHT FOR EVERYDAY LIFE SOLUTIONS

THE MAIN THEMES OF BOOK SERIES

DERIVATIVE KNOWLEDGE APPLIED TRUTH FROM NEW THOUGHT: A PRACTICAL GUIDE TO UNLOCKING TRUTH FROM NEW THOUGHT FOR EVERYDAY LIFE SOLUTIONS

'Derivative Knowledge Applied Truth from New Thought', a series that takes the profound insights of the 'Truth from New Thought' series and applies them to real-world problems.

This is not a series born out of mere contemplation or introspection, but rather, it is the result of rigorous scientific process and skill.

Drawing from the wellspring of knowledge in our original series, we've distilled and transformed these insights into practical guides. Each book in this series addresses a specific issue, such as insomnia or self-doubt, and provides actionable strategies grounded in the wisdom of 'Truth from New Thought'.

The genesis of this series lies in the recognition that the knowledge from 'Truth from New Thought' is not confined to the realm of philosophy. As demonstrated by the inclusion of 'Human Secret' in both the 'New Thought' and 'Psychology, Applied' categories of the National Library of Australia, the insights from our original series have practical, real-world applications. They transcend philosophical discourse and are firmly rooted in the principles of modern applied science.

"Derivative Knowledge Applied TRUTH FROM New Thought" series, we delve into the interplay between internal exploration and scientific acumen. The knowledge here is not just a powerful tool, but an essential instrument for genuine personal transformation, takes charge of your future and SOLVES various life problems on your own.

Here's to a future where we take responsibility for our own lives, armed with the power of applied *"TRUTH FROM New Thought"*.

'Skills in science' means 'the ability to uncover hidden laws in phenomena.'

'Scientific knowledge' means 'the laws that generate phenomena.'

The summary at the end of Chapter 3 'Read before the meaning of your life is lesser'. The foundational knowledge from the 'Truth from New Thought' series

Note: Knowledge references from the 'Truth from New Thought' series are used from the English language paperback version.

THE SECRETS OF INSOMNIA: SELF-TRAINING FOR HEALING,

INTRODUCTION

BUT WHY, DESPITE ADVANCED SCIENTIFIC KNOWLEDGE AND AN UNDERSTANDING OF THE CHEMICALS THAT REGULATE SLEEP AND WAKEFULNESS, DO WE STILL ENCOUNTER CHRONIC ISSUES WITH INSOMNIA? WHY DOES THIS PROBLEM PERSIST, EVEN WITH LONG-STANDING MEDICINAL TREATMENTS?

INTRODUCTION

Welcome to **"The Secrets of Insomnia: Self-Training for Healing,"** a book crafted from the commitment to apply the 'Truth from New Thought' in solving real-life problems. This volume specifically addresses the mystery of "The Secrets of Insomnia" and ways to self-train for overcoming sleeplessness.

This volume is an extension of the profound insights found in **"Human Secret:** Understanding Our Cosmic Connection," a cornerstone work that blends the realms of New Thought and Applied Psychology. And the results of the **'Skill of Creating Knowledge'** that are tried to be conveyed in the book *'Read before the meaning of your life is lesser'*

We are all well aware that good sleep is not just the foundation of good health, but also key to unlocking the full potential of our minds.

We know how a sleepless night can leave us exhausted, both physically and mentally, impairing our ability to think and function effectively the next day.

But why, despite advanced scientific knowledge and an understanding of the chemicals that regulate sleep and wakefulness, do we still encounter chronic issues with insomnia? Why does this problem persist, even with long-standing medicinal treatments?

What exactly is the "phenomenon" of insomnia?

"The Secrets of Insomnia" and the "Truth" created from 'Truth from New Thought' - what are they? And how can we develop self-training methods to escape the fate of sleeplessness that plagues many of us?

What is the ultimate disaster possible from insomnia? Will it remain a mystery to humanity post the inception of the new framework of thought inspired by the 'Truth from New Thought' series?

If we can train ourselves to address insomnia independently, what real-life skills will we acquire for our lives?

No matter who you are, regardless of whether you have had good or bad sleep experiences, we are confident that this book, with its foundation in 'Truth from New Thought,' will offer insights that can help you deal with this universal human issue of insomnia.This phenomenon will no longer be a mystery to us, and we can take control of our sleep quality ourselves, without the need for drugs or medication.

Let us embark on a journey to discover the real causes of our sleeplessness.

"If you find yourself unable to endure reading this book to the end, forcing yourself to read until you fall asleep, it means that the design of this book is correct and complete."

With Conscientious Responsibility,
Ekarach Chandon

Table of Contents

THE SECRETS OF INSOMNIA: SELF-TRAINING FOR HEALING,

1ST TOPIC:

"THE INVISIBLE CRISIS: RECOGNIZING THE UNSEEN THREATS TO OUR SOUL"

1ST TOPIC: "THE INVISIBLE CRISIS: RECOGNIZING THE UNSEEN THREATS TO OUR SOUL"

In a world bursting with data, both digital and sensory, we find ourselves drowning in an ocean of information.

Every day, a deluge of news, images, and sounds flood our senses, threatening to wash away the essence of who we are.

The challenge of our times is not just to stay afloat, but to find a way to navigate through this vast sea, discerning the truth from the myriad of falsehoods.

Yet, within this overwhelming tide, there's an invisible crisis looming - one that is silently eroding the very core of our being.

This unseen threat is not just a peril to our current existence but holds the power to haunt our souls even after our worldly departure.

The book 'Read Before the Meaning of Your Life is Lesser' offers a beacon of light in these treacherous waters. It speaks not just of the obvious, tangible problems we face, but delves deeper into the unseen challenges that confront our souls.

The book emphasizes the importance of discerning the genuine needs of our heart, rather than getting lost in the maze of endless desires and cravings.

For in succumbing to these unending wants, we risk becoming 'restless souls', tormented both in life and beyond.

1ST TOPIC:

Consider the profound truth encapsulated in this quote from the book: "In an era overloaded with information and a plethora of news, if we cannot revive such a skill, how are we to distinguish what is true from what is false? Reviving the human skill of 'Creating Knowledge' is paramount for people to maintain the essence of life. This allows us to independently discover what is true or false."

The sleepless nights, the torment of the restless soul, are not mere poetic expressions. They are grim realities for many, who, in their quest for more, have lost sight of their true self.

The pain of this loss, often, is felt more acutely in the stillness of the night, when the distractions of the day fade away.

What is this restless torment that keeps us awake? It's the suffering born out of unrecognized desires. These are not the desires we know of, but those deeply ingrained in our psyche, which we fail to acknowledge. To truly alleviate this suffering, we must first recognize it. Only then can our souls find the rest they so desperately seek.

But how do we begin this journey of self-awareness? The key lies in understanding and reviving the lost art of 'Creating Knowledge'. This skill, emphasized in 'Read Before the Meaning of Your Life is Lesser', is about discerning the intricate processes concealed within details.

It's about peeling back the layers, questioning the obvious, and seeking the truth that lies beneath.

1ST TOPIC:

"Don't let yourself become a restless soul at night merely because of endless cravings, to the point where we can't recognize the true suffering arising from our genuine desire."

For those who find themselves wandering in the dark, tormented by the unseen chains of their own making, there's hope.

Share this knowledge, embark on the journey of self-discovery, and light the way for others. For in understanding and confronting our true suffering, we not only find our own salvation but become beacons of hope for others lost in the storm.

Truth Quote:

"True comprehension of suffering is understanding our genuine needs, not blindly following what we think we want."

In these challenging times, let us not be passive consumers of information. Let's strive to be active seekers of truth, to recognize the unseen threats, and to ensure that our souls, both in this life and the next, are not left restless and tormented.

1ST TOPIC: YOUR NOTE

THE SECRETS OF INSOMNIA: SELF-TRAINING FOR HEALING,

2ND TOPIC:

THE FRAMEWORK OF THOUGHT THAT WILL BE USED TO STUDY THE PHENOMENON OF INSOMNIA AND TO CREATE TOOLS FOR SELF-PRACTICE TO SLEEP.

2ND TOPIC: THE FRAMEWORK OF THOUGHT THAT WILL BE USED TO STUDY THE PHENOMENON OF INSOMNIA AND TO CREATE TOOLS FOR SELF-PRACTICE TO SLEEP.

The preceding article aims to bring awareness to the causes of insomnia, drawing from the knowledge and thought frameworks presented in two books from the 'Truth from New Thought' series.

The first book, **"Human Secret: It's Time to Discern How We and the Universe are Intricately Connected,"** is recognized by the **National Library of Australia** in the categories of **'New Thought'** and **'Psychology, Applied'**. This categorization confirms the scientific process and skill employed in its writing.

The second book, **"Read Before the Meaning of Your Life is Lesser: Unlocking the Secrets to a Meaningful Existence,"** serves as the *foundational work for the entire series*, endeavoring to convey that the **'skill of creating knowledge'** is an inherent, fundamental trait within humans.

By employing the frameworks from these **two out of the five books** in the 'Truth from New Thought' series, we *can unravel the mystery of insomnia*. The thought processes from these books aid in uncovering the secrets of sleeplessness and in developing knowledge for self-training to treat this condition.

The following framework has been utilized:

2ND TOPIC:

The first framework is elucidated through Diagram 1 in Chapter 5, "Journey of Life," on page 46 of ***"Read Before the Meaning of Your Life is Lesser."*** It explains the factors that determine our life's fate.

Picture I. " What determines our destiny? "

Generally, our identity comprises observable elements within our minds, namely the layers of knowledge and thought.

A crucial sentence to consider in conjunction with this concept is

"The knowledge of others is just our data,"

from page 32 of the same book. It highlights that the information we continuously absorb throughout our life begins to shape our destiny unknowingly, residing in the layers of our understanding and thought.

2ND TOPIC:

 Without our awareness, *this information, derived from others' knowledge, transforms into either 'knowledge' or 'ignorance' within 'Us'*, consequently dictating our fate, such as the destiny of experiencing insomnia, as discussed in the first topic.

Diagram 2, from page 17 of "*Human Secret*," Secret 1st: ***The Secret of the Universe***, attempts to elucidate the components of the universe as a new thought framework. This conceptualization leads to a recognition of the crisis caused by an old understanding of the universe. The traditional concept of the universe leads to a critical point that reveals the paradox in human civilization's development, which we can begin to rectify on our own.

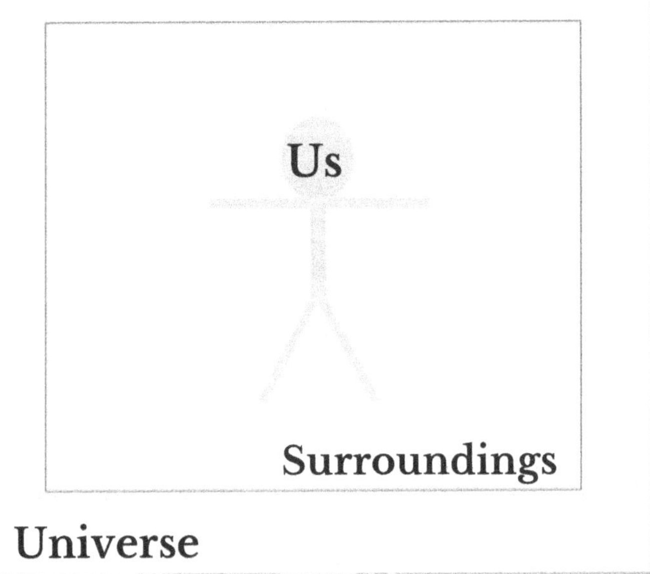

Picture 2. New thought ; Conceptual of the universe

2ND TOPIC:

Lacking this framework of thought in our considerations, we often cannot differentiate between problems and phenomena.

We tend to see problems as external environmental factors causing phenomena that impact us. In summary, from chapters 1 to 3, we deduce that:

Problems arise from "humans," while phenomena occur in the "environment."

The most effective way to solve problems, when we apply logic through language, reveals that the **best solution starts with our own acknowledgment of faults.** This is the succinct conclusion drawn from the second conceptual framework.

Regarding the **final Conceptual Diagram** before entering this topic, do not worry about the unfamiliar language or specialized terms, as they are elaborately explained in the primary books of the 'Truth from New Thought' series.

To thoroughly comprehend the cause of insomnia and accept it without doubt, one must understand the peculiar language in detail. You must read the full text on these transliterations in the main book of the Truth from New Thought series.

However, **if you seek immediate practical knowledge to address urgent problems like insomnia, the information provided here suffices**. Understanding the **'How to Self-Training for Healing'** in Topic 3 and applying this knowledge is certainly feasible.

2ND TOPIC:

For those curious about '**why**' the knowledge is presented in such a manner, a comprehensive understanding of every term referenced in the primary books is necessary. If intrigued by the 'why,' **delve deeper** by starting with the unfamiliar terms in table Annex IV: Ignorance Management in **Topic 4 of this book**, to begin uncovering answers from the five primary books of the 'Truth from New Thought' series.

As for **Diagram 3,** it is...

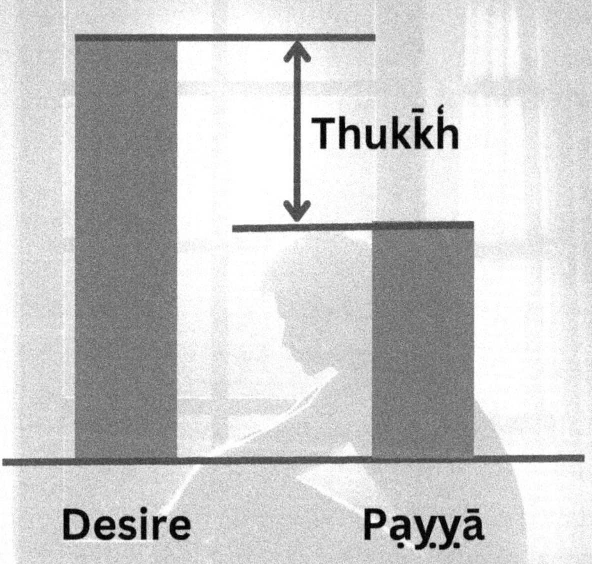

Picture 3. Picture showing the cause of "Thukīkh"

The **diagram** explains key concepts that alert us to whether we are experiencing a problem or are in a problematic phenomenon.

2ND TOPIC:

Key terms to understand in this context are '**Thukīkh**' and '**paẏyā**'. The diagram from page 82, Secret 7th: Why So Much Suffering? of "**Human Secret**," introduces these concepts.

In essence, 'Thukīkh' is defined for practical purposes as…

"*Thukīkh*"? It's the feeling of wanting.
The desire to have, the desire to be, the desire to own.

'*Paẏyā*', on the other hand, is defined as…
"The ability to see the world as it truly is."

This true world that we should perceive is essentially the **cause of our suffering**.

Thus, 'Thukīkh', translating to the feeling of wanting, the desire to have, to be, and to own, becomes a significant factor when we unknowingly let in various external **data into our minds**.

This data may consist of our own or others' knowledge or ignorance, unknowingly shaping our desires and wants.

To resolve this state, a considerable amount of 'paẏyā', developed through rigorous training, is necessary.

This is because we are unwittingly being controlled by '**Thoṣa**', which we will come to observe and understand in Topic 3, How to Self-Training for Healing.

2ND TOPIC:

From these three diagrams, we can conclude the cause of "insomnia" as unknowingly adopting others' ignorance as our own desires. This results in our '**Thoša**' remaining unresolved, continually influencing us because we haven't yet found the way back to fulfilling our original, true desires.

Each individual or soul must seek out their true original desires themselves.

The subsequent sections will provide a guide for training in this method

2ND TOPIC: YOUR NOTE

THE SECRETS OF INSOMNIA: SELF-TRAINING FOR HEALING,

3RD TOPIC:

3RD TOPIC: "HOW TO SELF-TRAINING FOR HEALING,"

Poses a vital question for our consideration: *If our sleeplessness isn't caused by external chemical factors or physical problems,* then **who or what is responsible for our sleep disturbance?**

In cases where sleeplessness isn't induced by external chemicals or actions, but we still find ourselves unable to sleep, we must question **who is generating these internal chemicals that disrupt our sleep**. If we continue to believe that external environments are the root of our problems, we might resort to using chemicals, drugs, or other stimulants to induce sleep, relying on external solutions rather than addressing the issue internally.

The true nature of insomnia often stems from an attempt to **resolve the unknown within our own body and mind**.

When we suppress this ignorance with chemicals, the unresolved issues accumulate, becoming more pronounced as we age. This accumulation of unresolved issues can prevent the realization of our deepest desires, leading to increased restlessness and sleeplessness at night. This phenomenon serves as a warning that becoming **'restless souls'** at night might not end even with the conclusion of our physical life.

The first article attempts to convey the **greatest danger of sleeplessness**: the risk of becoming 'restless souls' in the night. However, **do not let this fear prevent you from reading the articles that offer solutions.**

3RD TOPIC:

Explaining the utmost fear of sleeplessness is crucial for us to be clear and determined about how we wish to resolve our insomnia – whether we see the problem as stemming from the environment, relying on medications or chemicals, or whether we recognize that the issue lies within us and start to train ourselves for better sleep.

The **most terrifying** aspect of insomnia is the **"fear of going to sleep."** If this fear manifests subconsciously and becomes ingrained in us, treatment becomes increasingly challenging, requiring stronger medication.

This only adds to the accumulation of unresolved internal issues, leading to an explosive crisis at the end of life, where we experience the torment of being 'restless souls' at night.

Let's begin the journey of healing from insomnia and preventing the state of "fear of going to sleep." It's not too late to start. The first step is to adjust our mindset:

The current phenomenon of insomnia serves as a natural mechanism, prompting us to recognize that there is an issue within us (the problem of insomnia).

According to the conclusions drawn from Diagram 2, when we face a problem, it's an opportunity to introspect: **"Where are we going wrong in our lives?"**

3RD TOPIC:

Initiating this self-reflection before our time runs short is beneficial. It allows us to guide our remaining life back onto a path that fulfills our true, original desires. **This is the advantage for those who acknowledge their insomnia and accept that the problem lies within.**

The mechanism to navigate through insomnia, once its secret is understood, is straightforward:

Training to Align the 'Head/Ḥạwkhid' and 'Heart/Ḥạwcɪ':

PRE-SLEEP TRAINING

Preparing for sleep can be done in a variety of ways. As has been generally recommended, such as creating a sleep-conducive atmosphere, adhering to a regular bedtime, or addressing external environmental factors like lighting, sound, scent, humidity, temperature, or airborne chemicals in the bedroom.

Each person's external conditions differ, and while there may be similarities, customizing our environment without addressing the root causes within us does not provide an accurate solution.

We must question and recognize the differences in adjusting our environment for sleep among many people. Why do we struggle with sleeplessness despite these adjustments?

3RD TOPIC:

If the problem is similar – insomnia – but the advice for adjusting the environment differs, using the three conceptual frameworks and proper **"creating knowledge skill,"** we find that this issue is actually **about learning to accept what we have been denying or rejecting in our lives.**

Our inability to sleep when external conditions are not ideal is because our psyche is influenced by **'Thoša'** without our awareness, leading to a state of denial or rejection in our lives.

This denial or rejection, unchecked, grows to a point where it becomes a default mechanism, 'unknown' to us.

The outcome is an increased susceptibility to insomnia when environmental conditions do not align with our unrecognized denials.

Some might deny this, feeling they are easy-going with no significant life issues to reject. However, the very phenomenon of insomnia is a sign we must accept that there are aspects of our lives we are yet to acknowledge.

Therefore, the phase of preparing for sleep, which involves setting up the right environmental conditions, **must also include training ourselves to recognize and accept these hidden denials and rejections.**

This process is gradual, as the conditions for each individual to accept their external environment for sleep are unique.

3RD TOPIC:

By identifying these conditions ourselves, we significantly increase our chances of overcoming insomnia.

The practice of acknowledging that there are aspects of our lives we have not yet accepted, even if hidden, allows us to explore the ignorance concealed within the universe of our thoughts.

Once we address this ignorance and identify the conditions that make us accept our surroundings for sleep, we are ready to progress to the next stage.

3RD TOPIC:

SELF-TRAINING WHILE GOING TO SLEEP

WHEN IT'S TIME TO SLEEP, FOCUS ON OBSERVING THE TIP OF YOUR NOSE. NOTICE WHETHER YOUR MIND WILLINGLY OBSERVES THIS POINT. IF IT RESISTS, IT INDICATES THAT ''THOŠA' IS ACTIVE.

The activity of 'Thoŝa' serves as an indicator of how quickly we can overcome insomnia. If we can direct our thoughts to consistently observe the tip of our nose more swiftly and for longer durations, it suggests **an increased ease in falling asleep**. A key variable in this process is whether our sense of acknowledgment and the ability to recognize our faults become more evident each day. If the process of self-review improves and faults are identified quicker without deliberately controlling our thoughts - simply by letting them rest at the tip of the nose - and the acceptance of these faults becomes clear in our minds, it signifies that we are beginning to accept guidance from a source of information within us, beyond our brain.

In contrast, if directing our thoughts to the tip of our nose proves difficult, with thoughts either not arriving or only staying briefly, it is a sign that **'Thoŝa'** has deeply ingrained itself into our psyche. This deep-rooted habit, born from indulging our whims, becomes a significant obstacle. When even a short moment of control feels intolerable and any effort without immediate results is deemed unsuccessful, it indicates a profound influence of **'Thoŝa'** over our rational mind. To overcome this, one must practice persistently.

3RD TOPIC:

Practice involves directing the thoughts in our mind to observe the breath at the tip of our nose. If thoughts stray elsewhere, it shows that '***Thoṣa***' still holds sway, not yet conceding defeat and constantly seeking to prove itself right. To counter this, we must attempt to command our thoughts to acknowledge any faults made during the day, related or unrelated to the cause of insomnia. Finding and accepting our faults, once they surface in the language of our mind, and then guiding our thoughts back to the tip of the nose is key. If unsuccessful, release any frustration and try again.

Once you notice your thoughts resting at the tip of your nose, and if observed closely enough, another line of information becomes apparent - originating not from the '***Head/Ḥạwkhid***' but from the '***Heart/Ḥạwcɪ***'. Encountering this information means we are beginning to slow down '***Thoṣa***', preparing it to work alongside us. This discovery eases the process of identifying unacknowledged faults, propelling us toward accepting responsibility for them.

With each occurrence of insomnia, adjust your perspective to see it as an opportunity to review personal faults that hinder the fulfillment of our deepest desires. Don't focus on the time or how long you've been unable to sleep. Even if unable to sleep, consider it beneficial to rest with closed eyes. When following this method, the calmness brought about by observing the breath at the tip of the nose aids in uncovering our faults. Once these faults are acknowledged, sleep comes more easily, preventing us from becoming 'restless souls' in the night. Repeat this practice every night.

3RD TOPIC:

Bringing your thoughts to the tip of your nose, acknowledging faults, and recognizing the two lines of information originating from the '***Head/H̄ạwkhid***'and the '***Heart/H̄ạwcı***' - and doing so consistently - indicates successful training in managing 'thos'. This success means that when life presents challenges, our ability to review and identify our faults improves. Our chances of self-correction increase, leading to a life that fulfills our true desires, as we become capable of discerning them independently.

SELF-TRAINING FOR SLEEP: A PERSONAL JOURNEY

Bring your focus to the tip of your nose, accepting faults. Encounter two streams of information originating from the mind and heart. Repeat nightly, continually, until you begin to fall asleep on your own, without any symptoms of insomnia. This signifies successful self-training in managing 'Thoŝa.' If it remains challenging, find words to accompany your breath in and out, to command Tosa and observe thoughts at the tip of your nose.

For instance, in Buddhism, 'Phuth' while inhaling, 'Ṭho' while exhaling, or simply 'In' and 'Out' can be used. Additionally, those who can identify and rectify mistakes, discovering their true, original desire, can use this foundational desire to guide their breath.

3RD TOPIC:

For instance, in Buddhism, 'Phuth' while inhaling, 'Ṭho' while exhaling, or simply 'In' and 'Out' can be used. Additionally, those who can identify and rectify mistakes, discovering their true, original desire, can use this foundational desire to guide their breath.

Overcoming insomnia on your own, without external aid, marks successful Thoṡa self-training. When life challenges arise, you'll review faults faster than those untrained. Opportunities to correct oneself become easier. The destiny shaped by past mistakes diminishes, unveiling a life fulfilled in alignment with one's true desire, discernible to oneself.

The steps of Thoṡa self-training are detailed in the book "Read Before the Meaning of Your Life is Lesser," Chapter 9 - Self-Reflection While Reading Uncle's Book, which discusses buffalo training.

Detailed information can be found in the mentioned book.

3RD TOPIC:

Summarizing the entire phenomenon in such a narrative style, we can condense it into a How-To procedure as follows: Steps for Self-Training in Thoŝa for Achieving Sleep.

STAGES OF PRE-SLEEP TRAINING: EMBRACING INNER REALITIES AND EXTERNAL ENVIRONMENT

For preparing before going to bed, focusing on accepting and dealing with internal and external factors as follows:

1.**Accepting the truth:** *Accept that there are internal factors that we may not be aware of or accept that may affect the fate of our lives, such as appearing as a phenomenon of insomnia that occurs with our lives.*

2.**Adjusting the environment:** *While improving the external environment to help sleep, such as light, sound, smell, temperature, humidity, and chemicals in the bedroom, it is a matter to practice, find and accept that we have things that we do not accept hidden in our lives.*

3.**Understanding the differences in external factors:** *Realize that external factors suitable for sleep may vary in each individual because in fact the fate of each person's life has a life line that is not the same. What happens in life, what can be accepted in life, and what is not accepted in the life of each person is different. Finding information that tells you to do the same thing and then you can sleep the same is not a sustainable way for our individual insomnia problems.*

3RD TOPIC:

4.**Exploring internal denial:** *Understand that we have some denial or non-acceptance in our lives. Which small denials and accumulations are long-term non-acceptance, it is difficult to find to get in a hurry. But the clear result that causes us to not sleep is a phenomenon that really exists of the two things mentioned, both small denials that we do not see and the accumulation of non-acceptance in the fate of our lives that we do not accept for a long time.*

5. **Developing a sense of acceptance that we have things we do not accept hidden in the environment of the "data universe" we live in:** *Practice yourself to accept things that we do not feel or do not give importance to, things that we are more afraid of than enough to know that we do not accept. Through finding an environment that is not suitable for our sleep and then leaving the attachment to those unsuitable things out. In this step, the condition of the environment that makes us sleep will not occur until the "Self-Training While Going to Sleep" begins to work.*

6. **Searching for ignorance within the universe of thought:** *Search and deal with ignorance or non-acceptance hidden within our head/Ḥạwkhid. If we still can't sleep, we still can't find what we need to adjust the environment and "Self-Training While Going to Sleep" in the next topic. Can't proceed, it's a result that reflects that we still have ignorance hidden within the universe of our thoughts, go back and review, practice finding what we don't accept that we don't accept.*

<h1 style="text-align:center">3RD TOPIC:</h1>

7. ***Setting the conditions for a suitable environment:*** *Find the conditions for an external environment that makes us accept and can sleep easier. Passing all 6 steps, then enter this step, the result called success is that we can determine the environment that is suitable for sleeping by ourselves. And if the step of "Self-Training While Going to Sleep" works, it will make in this step, what we set, the environment that is suitable for our sleep, the conditions start to decrease, we will be able to go to bed, not afraid to go to bed, and sleep easier. The condition of insomnia when the environment is not suitable will disappear.*

Through these steps, we will be able to prepare ourselves for better quality sleep, not only focusing on external factors, but also including accepting and dealing with internal factors that may affect our sleep.

STAGES OF SELF-TRAINING WHILE GOING TO BED: A JOURNEY OF INNER ALIGNMENT AND RELAXATION

For preparing before going to bed, focusing on accepting and dealing with internal and external factors as follows:

1. **Acceptance and awareness of the problem:** Accept that the problem of insomnia comes from within us, not from the external environment or the use of chemicals to aid sleep.

2. **Attitude adjustment:** View the problem of insomnia as an opportunity to review and solve internal problems.

3RD TOPIC:

3.**Observing the breath before going to bed:** Watch the breath at the tip of the nose to create peace of mind and help us have mindfulness and tranquility.

4.**Identifying and accepting mistakes:** Use time before bed to review and accept mistakes or problems that may affect insomnia.

5.**Measuring Progress:** Working with using the measure that we order thoughts can be at the tip of the nose or cannot be at the tip of the nose is a sign that the level of our problem is still difficult as before or where is the development up in practice to heal oneself.

6.**Creating understanding and relationships between the mind and body:** Explore and create connections 'Head/H̄ạwkhid'and 'Heart/H̄ạwcı'.

7.**Using thoughts to create logic for oneself to accept mistakes:** Repeat this process every night by bringing thoughts back to the tip of the nose and accepting mistakes or flaws of oneself.

8.**Creating peace with observing the breath and using labels:** This step, I would like to expand to see clearly in the next subtopic.

9.**Continuous and regular practice:** Repeat this process continuously until you can sleep by yourself and reduce the dependence on chemicals or drugs.

3RD TOPIC:

Practicing these steps will help you cope with and solve the problem of insomnia by yourself, without having to rely on external help, such as using drugs or chemicals.

CREATING PEACE WITH OBSERVING THE BREATH AND USING LABELS:

While observing the breath at the tip of the nose, use labels to help focus. For example, use the word "in" when inhaling and "out" when exhaling, or use words according to your own beliefs or desires.

• For those who practice Buddhism, using the Buddhist word "Budd" and "Tho" while inhaling and exhaling is one option.

• For those who have reviewed and identified their original desires, they can create that desire into language and use it as a breath label.

• Measure the success of practice by the ability to bring thoughts to calm at the tip of the nose faster and longer.

3RD TOPIC:

REPETITION AND IMPROVEMENT:

• Practice this process continuously every night until you can sleep by yourself.

• If you still find it difficult to practice, try using labels to help control the mind and create more effective mindfulness.

• If the practice is successful, thoughts and acceptance of mistakes will appear clearly in the knowledge layer that is language, allowing us to observe and touch in the brain.

Practicing these steps will help you cope with insomnia on your own, without relying on external help. It also helps to create peace and mindfulness in the mind, which is an important factor in quality sleep and increases the ability to control the mind, which is a key to creating peace and mindfulness in the mind, and in preventing oneself from becoming 'restless souls' as mentioned.

For information on Thoša practice written in "Read Before the Meaning of Your Life is Lesser Chapter 9 Self-reflection while Reading Uncle's Book," you can read more details from that book to understand the practice guidelines more deeply.

3RD TOPIC:

GIVE IMPORTANCE TO THE PEACE THAT WILL BE FOUND FROM OBSERVING THE BREATH.

Self-training to be able to sleep is a way to help us understand ourselves and accept our mistakes more. When we can accept mistakes, we will be able to sleep without having to rely on any drugs or chemicals.

And finally, for How to Self-Training for Healing, leave the question as

If we have a problem, can't sleep, we will hope to rely on knowledge from whom

Between 1. People who have never had insomnia and suggest that people with insomnia take medication to sleep or 2. People who have insomnia and can train themselves to sleep by themselves

Hope that everyone who reads this book will become person number 2 who can help ourselves and others we love to escape from the condition 'restless souls' in the night in the future.

May everyone be lucky, sleep dreaming to know what the true desire of oneself is, after passing the condition of insomnia, everyone.

Uncle Mai Jaidi

3RD TOPIC: YOUR NOTE

THE SECRETS OF INSOMNIA: SELF-TRAINING FOR HEALING,

TAKE A BREAK BEFORE ENTERING TOPIC 4

NOTE: THE SOLUTION TO THE PROBLEM OF INSOMNIA IS NOT OVER YET. IF YOU FOLLOW THIS TOPIC AND SLEEP, IT MEANS THAT YOUR PROBLEM IS NOT VERY SERIOUS. BUT IF YOU DO IT UNTIL YOU ARE PROFICIENT AND STILL CAN'T SLEEP OR CAN'T FORCE YOURSELF TO DO IT, IT MEANS THAT YOUR INSOMNIA IS VERY SEVERE. YOU MUST STUDY IN THE NEXT TOPIC, TOPIC 4 IN DETAIL.

TAKE A BREAK BEFORE ENTERING TOPIC 4

for those who want to study in depth and wonder why it is like this. Start by understanding the ignorance that is a specific term used in the main book series 'Truth from New thought' from Section 4 These data "Ignorance Management" in the data to be presented next.

For those who still wonder how the mechanism that makes us sleepless is like this or wonder in controlling the head/Ḥawkhid why we can't do it, the result is difficult.

Can read the framework to study and create knowledge about the phenomenon of insomnia by yourself from all 3 books related to the problem area of insomnia. If you wish to be proficient, knowledgeable, or understand the deep mechanism, the three books consist of books 1, 2, and 5 from the book series Truth from New thought. Books 1 and 2 have been translated into English and are already on sale. The two books are

1st Truth from New thought. 'Read Before the meaning of your life is lesser: Unlocking the Secrets to a Meaningful Existence'

2nd Truth from New thought. 'Human Secret: It's time to discern how we and the universe are intricately connected'.

As for the 5th Truth from New thought book, it is not yet available in English at this time.

Understanding the Phenomenon of Insomnia Through 'Truth from New Thought'

TAKE A BREAK

If you're currently facing the challenge of insomnia, there's no need to worry. By taking responsibility for the problems we're facing right now, particularly those related to sleeplessness, we can begin to navigate back to a life free from insomnia, to return to the cause of having 'the karma of life that sleeps'.

The first two books in the 'Truth from New Thought' series are sufficient to gain a deep understanding and study the phenomenon of insomnia in our lives.

For those who seek more than just tools to aid in sleep, and have questions extending beyond the desire for immediate solutions, the book "The Secrets of Insomnia: Self-Training for Healing" from the series 'Derivative Knowledge Applied Truth from New Thought' is a valuable resource. It offers an opportunity to delve deeper into the 'Truth from New Thought' series.

Specifically, the upcoming Chapter 4 provides a comprehensive exploration into this subject.

By using our personal experiences with insomnia as a study tool, we can measure and examine whether 'Truth from New Thought' is practically applicable and effective, or if it is merely an elaboration of fanciful thoughts and words.

This guide serves as a practical manual for unlocking truths from new thought for real-life solutions.

TAKE A BREAK

CONTENTS THAT HAVE JUST BEEN READ IT CAN BE WRITTEN FOR EASY READING AS FOLLOWS.

Understanding Insomnia through 'Truth from New Thought' and Preparing for an In-Depth Study

1. Preparing for an In-Depth Study:

Before diving into Topic 4 for those who wish to study in depth, it's important to start by understanding the term 'ignorance' as used in the main 'Truth from New Thought' book series. Section 4, titled "Ignorance Management", is set to present data that will be essential for those wanting to delve deeper into the subject.

2. Mechanisms Behind Insomnia:

If you're curious about the mechanics of insomnia or why controlling the head/Ḥawkhid is challenging, You can read from the book related to the framework of thought that is used to create knowledge, this book "The Secrets of Insomnia: Self-Training for Healing," the framework of thought from all 3 books.

To gain proficiency and deep understanding, consider books 1, 2, and 5 from the 'Truth from New Thought' series. Books 1 and 2 are available in English:

TAKE A BREAK

Truth from New thought - Book 1: 'Read Before the meaning of your life is lesser: Unlocking the Secrets to a Meaningful Existence'

Truth from New thought - Book 2: 'Human Secret: It's time to discern how we and the universe are intricately connected'

The 5th book of the series is not yet available in English.

3. Dealing with Insomnia:

If you're currently facing the challenge of insomnia, there's no need to worry. By taking responsibility for the problems we're facing right now, which is still in the phenomenon of insomnia, to return to the cause of having 'the karma of life that sleeps' Truth from New thought, just books 1 and 2 are enough for us to understand deeply about ourselves and practice sincerely from the advice in both books. It will help us to study the phenomenon of our own insomnia.

And for those who have severe insomnia, Topic 4, which will be discussed in this book, is designed to start studying to solve the problem of severe insomnia, especially.

4. Beyond Immediate Solutions:

'The Secrets of Insomnia: Self-Training for Healing' from 'Derivative Knowledge Applied Truth from New Thought' is an excellent resource for those seeking more than just sleep aids.

TAKE A BREAK

The upcoming Topic 4 offers a deep dive into this subject, utilizing personal experiences with insomnia as a study tool.

This process helps to assess the practical applicability and effectiveness of 'Truth from New Thought', distinguishing it from mere fanciful elaborations.
The guide serves as a practical manual for unlocking truths from new thought for real-life solutions.

TAKE A BREAK NOTE

THE SECRETS OF INSOMNIA: SELF-TRAINING FOR HEALING,

BRAIN WARMING CONTENT BEFORE THE FOURTH TOPIC,

"PEOPLE WHO LIE TO THEMSELVES CANNOT ACCOMPLISH ANYTHING, AND THOSE WHO ARE DISHONEST CANNOT CURE DISEASES."'

BRAIN WARMING

WE NEED TO UNDERSTAND THE CORRECT KNOWLEDGE OF WORK OR PROBLEM-SOLVING, WHICH IS THE KNOWLEDGE OF TASK, PROCESS, SYSTEM. THIS KNOWLEDGE IS IN THE BOOK 'HUMAN SECRET' ANNEX III: THE FUNDAMENTAL OF HUMAN THOUGHT. WE DON'T HAVE TO WORRY ABOUT KNOWING EVERYTHING NOW FOR SOLVING THE PROBLEM OF INSOMNIA.

We should focus on the word 'Task' first because if the Task is not complete, the Process System will never be complete. We desire a complete process and system of sleep in our lives. The Task of good sleep must occur.

To consider what is the Task of good sleep, start by considering the language in the following two phrases:

'We want to sleep' or 2. 'We don't want to stay awake'
To find a complete Task in sleeping, we will find a Task that will be a complete measure from which phrase, 1 or 2.

For the answer that we are not fooled by the joke is the answer 'We don't want to stay awake' because if we do a small Task to prevent 'insomnia' from happening to us, our sleep will become a complete system.

Then when we consider from this phrase to find a Task that will be complete, we find that what we don't know is 'How does insomnia occur?' But we know that we don't want it. Therefore, to make our sleep system complete, we must create knowledge that 'What is insomnia?'"

BRAIN WARMING

Before considering what 'insomnia' is and what the smallest cause of its occurrence is, let's consider the text from the end of chapters 2 and 3 of the book 'Read Before the meaning of your life is lesser'.

At the end of chapter 2, it says,

'All languages are merely symbols that hide true relationships behind them.'

At the end of chapter 3, it says,

'Skills in science' means 'the ability to uncover hidden laws in phenomena.'

'Scientific knowledge' means 'the laws that generate phenomena.'

The example that tells us that language is just a symbol, and even though we have the language that is a symbol that says what scientific skills are, it doesn't mean we become scientifically skilled.

If it were easy to know the language and symbols, then we could become like the great scientists of the past. But in reality, it's not like that.

Language is just a symbol that hides the true relationships behind it.

BRAIN WARMING

The language that says 'Skills in science' means 'the ability to uncover hidden laws in phenomena.' also has a hidden relationship behind it. Can we use our skills according to this language?

If we can, and we want to sleep, we have to prevent ourselves from encountering phenomena that make us sleepless. Do we know what the hidden law that causes insomnia is? Then we won't interfere with the law that causes the phenomenon, the one that causes insomnia.

But if we can't, we still have the problem of insomnia. It means we don't have this knowledge in our information system, in our head. We still can't create knowledge about what law or what is hidden in nature that makes us sleepless.

Let's consider the following phenomenon to see what is hidden in insomnia.

'Suppose on a comfortable day in our youth, we are sleeping on our happy rest day. The sleep is going very happily, full of happiness and comfort. Then the sun rises, the alarm clock rings. The cartoon that we want to watch is on time, we can watch it now. Or our parents have an appointment to take us out of the house

What happens to us? We yawn and get up, or even if we can get up quickly, one thing that works to make us get up, which we command, is called ''Thoṣa'.' We command ''Thoṣa'' to wake up all our information systems to work according to our command.'

BRAIN WARMING

The small point that we can observe from this story tells us about the existence of 'data,' one characteristic that works with 'Us'. 'data' that commands us to wake up, that data is called "Thoṣa'.' This word comes up again.

When we clearly see that we use 'Thoṣa' to wake us up, which is equivalent to insomnia, we cannot use that 'Thoṣa' to command us to sleep.

The time when we are asleep is because we command 'Thoṣa' or 'Thoṣa' commands us when we can no longer do so.

If you have read up to Topic 4, there will be many unexplained technical terms in this book. You don't need to worry about them. Just focus on one word, 'Thoṣa'.

'Thoṣa' is one of the 'Kileṣ' that Buddha discovered and actually works in our life system. Anyone who has read the book up to this topic and has felt frustrated, annoyed with the language they don't understand, the text that is written in circles, the content that is repeatedly described, and makes it difficult to finish reading, difficult to understand, raises questions that if you observe yourself in detail, you will know that you ask why not write easier to read, don't understand, want to stop reading, it shows the existence of 'Thoṣa'.

If we have symptoms in the group of symptoms mentioned and can accept that we are like that, it means that now we know a little bit that the information that is one of the 'Kileṣ' is working with the mechanism that makes us sleepless without our command, that is 'Thoṣa.'

BRAIN WARMING

Therefore, the natural law that makes us wake up or sleepless is "The Kileš 'Thoša' receives a command either by us consciously or by Thoša commanding unconsciously."

In simple language for those who have studied the Kileš clearly is "Thoša works." It then makes us sleepless.

How does it work?

'Thoša' works because there is something that denies, does not accept, exists in our system. 'Thoša' works by 'Thoša'.

Then 'Thoša' works because there is something waiting to be received as information in our system. 'Thoša' works by Lopha. Lopha is the desire that is not responsible.

Then we have something we want, but what we get is not like what we want, which is our ideal. 'Thoša' works by Moha. Moha is not knowing what we don't know that exists in the information system, both in the head, in life, and in our hearts.

All three mechanisms are the laws that make us sleepless. If summarized to understand more easily, our life is played by Kileš.

Played by the mechanism according to the natural law that wants us to return to the path of life that does not sleep, does not fall into the karma 'the karma of life that sleeps.' A life that sleeps is a life that does not think responsibly for the true meaning of one's life.

BRAIN WARMING

Kileŝ , which protect ourselves, are therefore drawn to work to make us sleepless so that we have the opportunity to review this karma and get out of this karma of ours.

For those who have read up to this point and can accept this truth, I would like to recommend reading the book 'Read Before the meaning of your life is lesser' to review and design a new karma of ourselves. Get out of the karma of sleeplessness that we are played by from the set of knowledge and ignorance of others that live in our head, in our life, in our heart.

Returning to the content of sleep, when we have the hidden law that makes us sleepless, what remains is to practice not to let that law happen to us again. Complete sleep occurs to us.

'Thinking is Comparing' - The Undeniable Truth. From Annex III: The Fundamental of Human Thought? The book Human Secret.

This book is designed this way so that we can see our Thoŝa defilement that occurs in our thinking system all the time that there is a comparison happening in our brain.

Practice according to the instructions in this book, read the whole book several more times for understanding and to be a guide for your life to have a complete sleep system.

BRAIN WARMING

THINKING IS COMPARING. LET'S READ IN ANOTHER WAY THAT I TRIED TO ORGANIZE FOR EASY READING.

BRAIN WARM-UP BEFORE TOPIC 4: UNDERSTANDING 'TASK' IN INSOMNIA

Self-Deception and Success:

- "One cannot succeed in any task nor effectively heal a condition by being dishonest or deceiving oneself."

- Before tackling the final and most challenging stage of addressing severe insomnia, it's crucial to have the correct knowledge about solving problems. This involves understanding 'Task,' 'Process,' and 'System,' as elaborated in the book "Human Secret" Annex III: The Fundamental of Human Thought. However, for resolving insomnia issues, focus primarily on 'Task'.

The Importance of 'Task':

- The concept of 'Task' is essential because if the task is incomplete, the process and system cannot be fully realized. Our desire is to achieve a complete process and system for a good night's sleep, and thus the 'Task' of good sleep must be established.

BRAIN WARMING

Determining the 'Task' for Quality Sleep:

- Consider these two expressions:
    1. "I want to sleep."
    2. "I do not want to experience insomnia."

- To find a complete 'Task' for effective sleep, decide which expression better represents the goal: 1 or 2.

- The less influenced answer by impulsiveness is "I do not want to experience insomnia." Preventing the occurrence of insomnia, even on a small scale, leads to a complete system for sleep.

Identifying the Task:

- *Upon reflecting on the second expression to identify the 'Task' for completeness, it's realized that what is unknown is "how insomnia occurs." Knowing that we do not want insomnia, to complete our sleep system, we must develop an understanding of what "insomnia" truly is.*

BRAIN WARMING

Understanding 'Insomnia' and Its Fundamental Task

Considering 'Insomnia' and Its Smallest Cause:

- Before delving deeper into the phenomenon of insomnia and its smallest causative 'Task', let's reflect on the statements from the end of chapters 2 and 3 of the book 'Read Before the meaning of your life is lesser':

- **End of Chapter 2:**

    - *"All languages are merely symbols that hide true relationships behind them."*

- **End of Chapter 3:**

    - *"Skills in science" means "the ability to uncover hidden laws in phenomena."*

    - *"Scientific knowledge" means "the laws that generate phenomena."*

BRAIN WARMING

Language, Science, and Reality:

- Language is just a symbol, with the truth of relationships hidden behind it. Knowing the language of 'scientific skills' doesn't automatically endow one with those skills. If it were so simple, the world would be abundant with eminent scientists, but reality says otherwise.

- Similarly, understanding the phrase "Skills in science" means more than just recognizing words; it involves uncovering the hidden relationships and applications behind these skills.

- If we want to sleep well, we must prevent phenomena that lead to insomnia by understanding the hidden laws that cause it. If we are still experiencing insomnia, it indicates a lack of this knowledge in our mental system. We haven't yet deciphered the rules hidden in nature causing our sleeplessness.

BRAIN WARMING

Examining a Relatable Scenario:

- Consider this scenario: On a relaxing day, while we are deeply asleep, enjoying a peaceful rest, several triggers might wake us up, like a rising sun, an alarm clock, an awaited cartoon show, or a planned outing with parents.

- What happens to us in these moments? We may wake up groggily or jump out of bed rapidly. This awakening is orchestrated by a force we call 'Impulse' or 'Thoṣa.' We command 'Thoṣa' to activate our entire data system to function as per our instruction. This small observable instance from the story reveals the existence of a certain type of 'Data' that works with us - 'Data' that commands us to wake up. Let's call this data 'Thoṣa' once again.

Addressing 'Thoṣa' before Diving into Topic 4

Focusing on 'Thoṣa':

- As you've journeyed through this book to Topic 4, you might have encountered numerous untranslated terms. However, it's essential to focus on just one term: 'Thoṣa'.

- 'Thoṣa' is one of the defilements ('kilesas') discovered by the Buddha and operates within our life's data system. If you've felt frustrated or annoyed by the complex language, the roundabout narratives, and the repetitive, hard-to-follow content, raising questions like "Why isn't this written more straightforwardly?"—these are indications of 'Thoṣa' at work.

BRAIN WARMING

Understanding 'Thoṡa':

- 'Thoṡa' is active when we experience feelings of annoyance or difficulty in understanding the content. It operates due to our rejection or non-acceptance of certain aspects within our system. 'Thoṡa' functions either due to our conscious command or unconsciously.

- In simple terms for those familiar with the concept of 'kilesas', 'Thoṡa' is the reason we experience insomnia.

How Does 'Thoṡa' Work?

- 'Thoṡa' operates because there are things we reject or do not accept within our system. It can also be triggered by desires or expectations that enter our system.

- If what we receive differs from our ideal or desired outcome, 'Thoṡa' operates through 'Moha' (ignorance or delusion) – the lack of awareness of our unknowns in the data system of our mind, life, and heart.

- These three mechanisms constitute the natural laws causing our insomnia. Summarizing, our life is affected by these 'kilesas', guiding us away from a 'life that sleeps'—a life unaware of its true purpose. 'Thoṡa' disrupts our sleep to allow us to reflect on and escape this fate.

BRAIN WARMING

Realization and Application:

- "When we clearly see that we use 'Thoša' to wake us up, which is equivalent to insomnia, we cannot use that 'Thoša' to command us to sleep. The time when we are asleep is because we command 'Thoša' or 'Thoša' commands us when we can no longer do so."

- This realization is crucial in understanding our relationship with sleep and insomnia. It highlights the importance of being aware of how 'Thoša' operates within us. Recognizing this dynamic is the first step in regaining control over our sleep patterns.

Next Steps for Readers:

- If you've reached this point and accept this truth, I recommend reading 'Read Before the meaning of your life is lesser' to reassess and redesign your destiny away from the fate of insomnia.

- The book is designed to reveal our 'Thoša', which constantly operates in our thought system through comparisons.

- Revisit the book multiple times for deeper understanding and to use it as a guide for achieving complete sleep systems in your life.

BRAIN WARMING

'Thinking is Comparing' – The Core Concept:

- From 'Human Secret' Annex III: The Fundamental of Human Thought ?, this book is structured to expose our 'Thoša', evident whenever we make comparisons in our minds.

- Practice as advised in this book. Re-read it several times to understand and make it a guide for your life to achieve a complete sleep system.

BRAIN WARMING

The Journey's End: A Reflection on Embracing the Tools Within

As we reach the conclusion of this journey, I invite you to revisit and fully engage with all the tools provided in this book.

Remember, if the reading becomes overwhelming, if the end seems elusive, persist. Read and re-read, repeatedly and patiently. If mastering the breath still eludes you, train your 'Thoša' to bring you back to these pages. For if you can command the reading but find it challenging to complete, falling asleep before the end, it signifies that the design of this book, in battling insomnia, has achieved its purpose in full.

As we part ways, I bestow upon you a blessing of fortune, to encounter the causes that awaken your 'Thoša', that stir your restlessness. Each person's journey, unique in its awakening, calls for introspection.

For the women among my readers, it might be matters of forgiveness yet to be fully embraced, or perhaps a yearning to return to the comforting embrace of a beloved mother. We choose our birth, drawn to those we love profoundly, yearning for one more night of tender closeness, recognizing that the nights spent cradled in our mother's arms were far too few.

For the men, your destiny is yours to uncover, beginning with the acceptance that this life was chosen out of desire, out of want. Perhaps, one day, you'll be fortunate enough to discern the exact fate that disrupts your sleep that awakens you to another life within this very existence.

BRAIN WARMING NOTE

TOPIC 4: IGNORANCE MANAGEMENT

THE BOOK 'THE SECRETS OF INSOMNIA: SELF-TRAINING FOR HEALING' IS CREATED FROM THE FRAMEWORK OF THOUGHT OF THE BOOKS 'TRUTH FROM NEW THOUGHT' VOLUME 1 AND VOLUME 2. THEREFORE, IT REFERS TO 'IGNORANCE MANAGEMENT' FROM THE BOOK 'HUMAN SECRET: IT'S TIME TO DISCERN HOW WE AND THE UNIVERSE ARE INTRICATELY CONNECTED' VOLUME 2.

TOPIC 4: IGNORANCE MANAGEMENT

And from the uncle's knowledge that gives us from the previous Annex, Annex 3 "Thinking is comparing" If the uncle's knowledge is not just our information that has been read, received, to the effort to transmit all the skills from the uncle through the book. Come 2 volumes already until we can touch that

"**Thinking is comparing**" is not just as this text says "*The knowledge of others is just our data*" This knowledge of the uncle is a **truth** that we can **touch** already.

If so, we really feel that "**Thinking is comparing**" and "**All languages are merely symbols that hide true relationships behind them.**" Managing ignorance that arises from "obstacles in the knowledge level through language" should not be difficult.

For the uncle, 'Ignorance Management' is far more important than 'Knowledge Management', especially for individuals who wish to discover the meaning of their own lives through their own knowledge.

TOPIC 4: IGNORANCE MANAGEMENT

'Ignorance Management' is of utmost importance if we choose to have that responsibility in our life.

What the uncle will facilitate is to compile the Codex Transliteration Table of these words, where it appears, from the first book in the Truth from New thought series to the latest book we are reading now, Human Secret. To allow us to trace back to the meaning of the symbols that are obstacles, from the first use, where is it located, in what issue, in the truth from New thought from these books that the uncle wrote.

TOPIC 4: IGNORANCE MANAGEMENT

Codex Transliteration Table; **First book** of the *'Truth from New Thought'* *series*, the book **'Read Before the meaning of your life is lesser'**.

DIACRITIC TRANSLITERATION	THAI	THAI ROMANIZATION	PAGE
Rû ṣụk	รู้สึก	Rusuek	26
sìng thỉ rûṣụk	สิ่งที่รู้สึก	Sing Thi Rusuek	26
rû̂	รู้	Ru	34
khid	คิด	Khit	34
moħa	โมหะ	Moha	35
thoṡa	โกสะ	Thosa	35
Mịmī šti	ไม่มีสติ	Mai Mi Sati	48
mī šti	มีสติ	Mi Sati	48
<u>šti</u>	สติ	Sati	50
Kileš	กิเลส	Kilet	51
Ṣrạthṭhā	ศรัทธา	Sattha	60
Tạw rûṣụk	ตัวรู้สึก	Tua Rusuek	84
ħạwkhid	หัวคิด	Huakhit	85
ħạwcı	หัวใจ	Huachai	85
Pạy̯y̯ā	ปัญญา	Panya	97

TOPIC 4: IGNORANCE MANAGEMENT

Codex Transliteration Table; **First book** of the *'Truth from New Thought'* *series*, the book **'Read Before the meaning of your life is lesser'**.

DIACRITIC TRANSLITERATION	THAI	THAI ROMANIZATION	PAGE
Lopha	โลภะ	Lo Pha	115
Jaidee	ใจดี	Chaidi	139
Phrĥmwiĥãr 4	พรหมวิหาร สี่	Phromwihan 4	139
Mettā	เมตตา	Metta	139
Kruṇā	กรุณา	Karuna	139
Muthitā	มุทิตา	Muthita	139
Xubekkhā	อุเบกขา	Ubekkha	139
Cit	จิต	Chit	140
Šwa	สวะ	Sawa	165
Thukkh́	ทุกข์	Thuk	175
šukh́	สุข	Suk	175
Khwāmlap khǫ̃ng khon	ความลับของคน	Khwam Lap Khong Khon	206

TOPIC 4: IGNORANCE MANAGEMENT

Codex Transliteration Table; **Second book** of the *'Truth from New Thought'* series, the book **'Human Secret'**.

DIACRITIC TRANSLITERATION	THAI	THAI ROMANIZATION	PAGE
Rûṡụk	รู้สึก	Rusuek	18
Khid	คิด	Khit	18
Rû	รู้	Ru	18
Kileš	กิเลส	Kilet	18
Ŝìng thì rûṡụk	สิ่งที่รู้สึก	Sing Thi Rusuek	19
Thukkḣ	ทุกข์	Thuk	22
Ḥạwkhid	หัวคิด	Huakhit	25
ḥạwcı	หัวใจ	Huachai	25
Tạw rûṡụk	ตัว รู้สึก	Tua Rusuek	27
Pạyyā	ปัญญา	Panya	41
Lopha	โลภะ	Lo Pha	47
thoša	โทสะ	Thosa	47
moḥa	โมหะ	Moha	47
Cit	จิต	Chit	62
Mī ḥạwcı	มี หัวใจ	Mi Huachai	112

TOPIC 4: IGNORANCE MANAGEMENT

Codex Transliteration Table; **Second book** of the *'Truth from New Thought'* series, the book **'Human Secret'**.

DIACRITIC TRANSLITERATION	THAI	THAI ROMANIZATION	PAGE
mī ḥạwkhid	มี หัวคิด	Mi Huakhit	131
Čhạntha	ฉันทะ	Chantha	133
Tạṇhā	ตัณหา	Tanha	133
Rūp	รูป	Rup	147
nām	นาม	Nam	147
Jaidi	ใจดี	Chaidi	161
Mịmī šti	ไม่มี สติ	Mai Mi Sati	186
mī šti	มี สติ	Mi Sati	187
Šti	สติ	Sati	188

TOPIC 4: IGNORANCE MANAGEMENT

And the combined Codex Transliteration Table for the **'Truth from New Thought'** book series is as follows:

DIACRITIC TRANSLITERATION	1 ST BOOK	2ND BOOK
Rû šụk	26	18
šìng thî rûšụk	26	19
rû	34	18
khid	34	18
moħa	35	47
thoša	35	47
Mịmī šti	48	186
mī šti	48	187
<u>šti</u>	50	188
Kileš	51	18
Șraṭhṭhā	60	-
Ṭaw rûšụk	84	27
ħạwkhid	85	25
ħạwcı	85	25
Pạyyā	97	41

TOPIC 4: IGNORANCE MANAGEMENT

And the combined Codex Transliteration Table for the **'Truth from New Thought'** book series is as follows:

DIACRITIC TRANSLITERATION	1 ST BOOK	2ND BOOK
Lopha	115	47
Jaidi	139	161
Phrṅmwiñār 4	139	-
Mettā	139	-
Kruṇā	139	-
Muthitā	139	-
Xubekk̄hā	139	-
Cit	140	62
Šwa	165	-
Thukk̄ḥ	175	22
šuk̄h	175	-
Khwāmlap khǭng khon	206	-
Mī ḥạwci	-	112
mī ḥạwkhid	-	131
Čhạntha	-	133

TOPIC 4: IGNORANCE MANAGEMENT

And the combined Codex Transliteration Table for the **'Truth from New Thought'** book series is as follows:

DIACRITIC TRANSLITERATION	1 ST BOOK	2ND BOOK
Taṇhā	-	133
Rūp	-	147
nām	-	147

Truth from New thought

1st Book; **Read Before the meaning of your life is lesser**

2nd Book; **Human Secret**

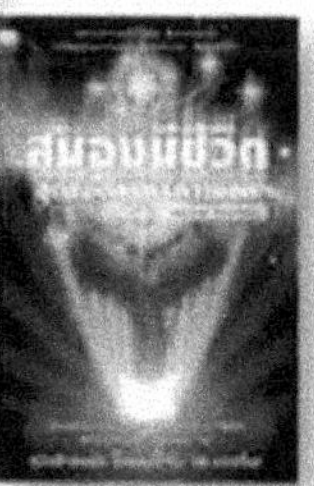

TOPIC 4: YOUR NOTE

THE SECRETS OF INSOMNIA: SELF-TRAINING FOR HEALING,

SPECIAL SECTION: EMBRACING RESPONSIBILITY AND TRUTH

STRICT WARNING: DO NOT READ THIS SECTION FIRST!

IF YOU JUMP DIRECTLY TO THIS SECTION WITHOUT THOROUGHLY READING AND UNDERSTANDING THE PRECEDING CONTENT, YOU WILL MISS CRUCIAL INSIGHTS AND GUIDANCE ESSENTIAL FOR FULLY GRASPING AND BENEFITING FROM THIS INFORMATION. THIS WARNING IS IN PLACE TO PROTECT YOU FROM MISUNDERSTANDINGS AND INCOMPLETE APPLICATION, WHICH COULD LEAD TO OUTCOMES NOT AS ANTICIPATED.

THE FINAL TOPIC

If you've made it to this **The final Topic** without having read the preceding content, be warned: **the ability of this book to assist you will be nearly null.**

If '**Thoṣa**' is keeping you from accepting this truth, and '**Moha**' is preventing you from acknowledging that others may know something you don't, then these insights won't be able to aid you in finding restful sleep.

However, if you've familiarized yourself with '**Thoṣa**' and the denial of unknown knowledge, the upcoming truths rooted in natural laws behind sleeplessness can still work for you.

Don't deny that these truths are real.

Truly, the knowledge herein about the phenomenon of insomnia, caused by '**Kileṣ**' at work within us, is what this next part is all about.

THE FINAL TOPIC

The final Topic, 'The Secrets of Insomnia: Self-Training for Healing,' reveals just this:

The secret of insomnia:

*Our lives are stirred awake by '**Kileš**' because there are unresolved issues - 'the karma of life that sleeps' - turning us into 'restless souls at night.' It's waiting for us to resolve.*

Self-Training for Healing:

'Humans must acknowledge their faults and use their thoughts to strive for taking responsibility for their own lives.'

This book is designed to help you encounter your own 'Thoša' and learn to manage it. It serves as a tool to improve your sleep. If you find yourself unable to finish reading this book or falling asleep before the end, it means that the book is effectively working as intended.

THE FINAL TOPIC NOTE

THE VIDEO CLIPS RELATED TO SLEEP TRAINING ON THE EKARACH CHANDON YOUTUBE CHANNEL:

019 OFFICIALE7 SLEEP TRAINING VERSION; "THE SECRETS OF INSOMNIA":

- CLIP FOR SLEEP TRAINING

021 EXTENDED 'DEEP SLEEP TRAINING' INSPIRED BY 'THE SECRETS OF INSOMNIA':

- CLIP FOR EXTENDED DEEP SLEEP TRAINING
- FOR DATA ALIGNMENT IN ME/CFS PATIENTS

THE FINAL TOPIC NOTE

THE FINAL TOPIC NOTE

THE FINAL TOPIC NOTE

THE FINAL TOPIC NOTE

THE FINAL TOPIC NOTE